Knowing Me From A to Z

A Child's Mindset

**Harry Petsanis
Donna McCance**

Copyright 2022

Harry Petsanis and Donna McCance

All rights reserved.

No part of this publication may be reproduced in any form, or by any means, electronic or mechanical, including photocopying, recording, or any information browsing, storage or retrieval system, without permission in writing from the authors.

Dedication

This book is dedicated to all children so they can develop their individual mindset of being true to who they are, learn to know and trust their instincts, and choose the path that they know is best for them.

Harry Petsanis and Donna McCance

Table of Contents

Introduction	**1**
Knowing Me From A to Z	**2**
Notes and Vocabulary	**15**
Mindset Words and Sentences	**41**
About the Authors	**68**

Introduction

"Knowing Me From A to Z" was written as a starting point to create change in behaviors so that children will be allowed to develop their independent, free thinking and individualistic mindset through their own self-awareness. As adults step back and allow children to develop self-awareness, only then will children be empowered to take ownership of their learning and their lives.

This book was designed to integrate reading with engaging children in meaningful conversations. The key strategy for reading this book involves asking and answering questions to stimulate and enhance conversations. Encourage children to ask questions and allow them time to reflect and absorb so they can **formulate their own answers.**

This book was also written with the intent to reach different learning levels within the defined age of a child, understanding that there are different levels of learning within the range of birth until eighteen years of age. However, it was also written with the intent that any adult, regardless of age, may benefit from the content.

Text complexity and rich vocabulary challenge children to read, hear, and say things with diversity.

A, B

I want you to know all about me,

And who I am so you can see,

I'm bold and bright, boisterous and free,

And awesome, as I was born to be.

C, D

I will control, what I can do.

Chart my course and changes too.

Make decisions, not based on you.

I'll determine, what is untrue.

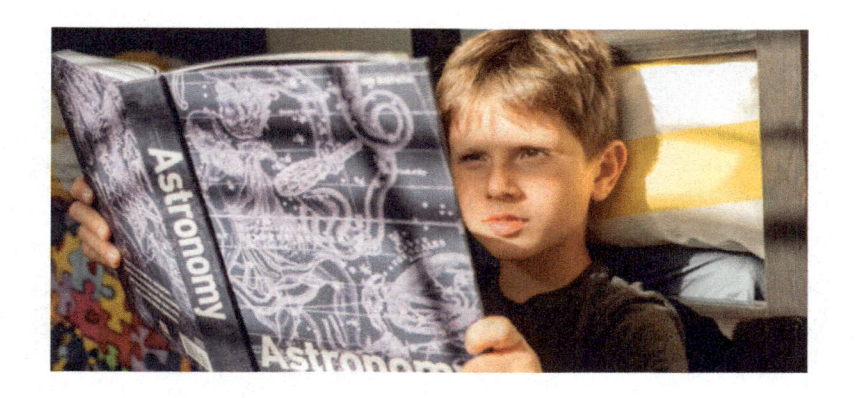

E, F

I'm always **e**ager, to seek and **f**ind,

Some **f**acts and truths, to **f**ill my mind.

Never say, I'll **f**all behind.

I'm **e**mpowered to be, as I'm designed.

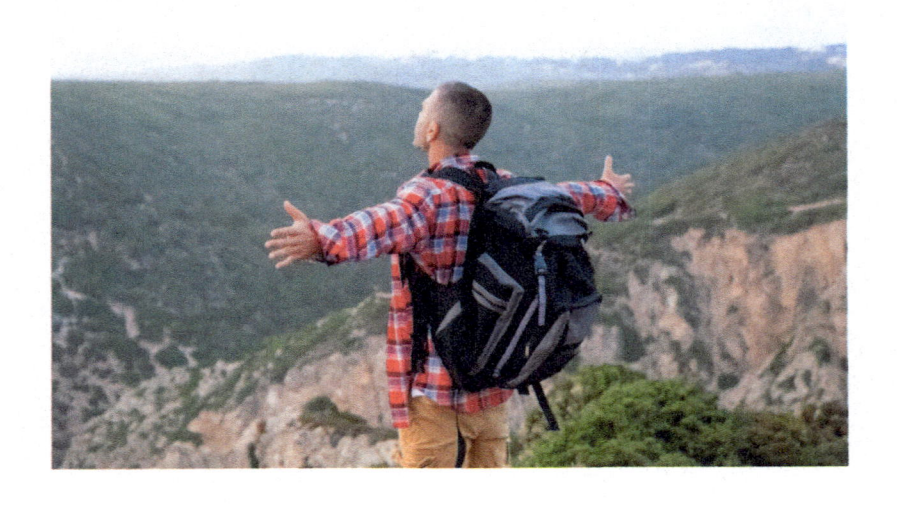

G, H

Do not deny my chance to **g**row.

Give me space,

my thoughts will flow.

I don't need to **h**ear all you know.

I know myself from **h**ead to toe.

I, J

It's okay, it's just a mistake.

I'm on a journey, things will break.

The path to joy, is mine to take.

My imagination, I will not forsake.

K, L

Be **k**ind to me, that's how I **l**earn,

Kindness to others, I will return.

The **k**indling in me, will always burn.

Don't dim my **l**ight, it's now my turn.

M, N

I have to be **m**e, don't hold **m**e back.

No **n**eed to say what you think I lack.

Not everything, is white and black.

I'll keep **m**y train, on the track.

O, P

Opinions of me have already been stated.

I don't need to be judged, or berated.

My life can't be planned, or orchestrated.

The restrictive process is so antiquated.

Q, R

Slow or **q**uick, it's my pace to decide.

I didn't ask you to come for the **r**ide.

This is my **q**uest, I don't need a guide.

Remember this, I won't be denied.

S, T

Don't force me to do all these things,

Or make me jump, when the bell rings.

I'm not a puppet, held by strings.

Let me be me, as my own heart sings.

U, V

Understand me. I'm very smart.

The ultimate goal, is an unfiltered heart.

I don't need, to play a part.

The uniVerse is where I'll start.

W, X

I want to know me, know me too.

Everything isn't all about you.

Be eXtra careful of

what you say and do.

I'm eXtraordinary! Will you get a clue?

Y, Z

I **y**earn to learn, I have the **z**eal.

Release **y**our grip, I've got the wheel.

Reali**z**e this, to which I appeal.

The road is mine, not **y**ours to steal.

Notes

VOCABULARY

A, B

Bold: not afraid to take risks, brave

Bright: intelligent, smart, cheerful

Boisterous: having lots of energy

Free: able to act or do as one wants

Awesome: extremely good

Notes

C,D

Control: not able to act or do as you want

Chart: map or plan

Course: path

Changes: doing something different

Determine: thinking about what you want to do

Decisions: what it is you want to do

Untrue: not real; lie

Notes

E, F

Eager: wanting to do something very much

Facts: something true, proven, or correct

True: what you instinctively know to be a fact

Instinctively: what you feel to be true

Empowered: giving yourself the power to do something

Designed: how something was meant to be

Notes

G, H

Deny: to refuse, prevent, not allow

Grow: develop, learn

Thoughts: what you are thinking

Notes

I, J

Mistake: learning

Journey: going from one place to another

Joy: doing what you love and being who you are

Path: the way

Imagination: the ability to be creative

Forsake: not give up on

Notes

K, L

Kindling: source of fire

Kindness: open, caring heart

Dim: less bright

Burn: on fire

Notes

M, N

Lack: something missing

Black: one of many colors

White: one of many colors

Train: railroad car used for transportation

Track: a path that leads in a direction

Notes

O, P

Opinion: what someone thinks

Judgments: someone's opinion based on their feelings

Antiquated: old, outdated

Berated: words used to hurt us

Planned: already decided

Orchestrated: directed, controlled

Restrictive: limit and control someone's freedom

Process: way of doing things

Notes

Q, R

Pace: time and speed it takes to do something

Decide: making up your mind

Quest: journey

Guide: leading and showing the way

Denied: rejected, something someone keeps from you

Notes

S, T

Force: made to do something you don't want to do

Puppet: a figure moved by someone with their hand

Jump: move quickly

Strings: material used to attach things

"As my heart sings": being yourself, doing what you want

Notes

U, V

Ultimate: highest, final

Unfiltered: original, not changed

Universe: the entire cosmic system

Notes

W, X

Extra: more than usual

Extraordinary: above and beyond

Careful: aware, cautious

Clue: information

Notes

Y, Z

Yearn: strong desire or want

Zeal: really wanting to do something

Release: to let go

Realize: to become aware of something

Appeal: a serious request

Steal: to take something that belongs to someone else

Mine: BELONGS TO ME!

Mindset Words and Sentences from A to Z

The following pages include challenging "Mindset Words from A to Z" to help to children and adults develop an understanding of language that can reflect mindset and actions in positive ways.

These words were put into sentences to allow for an understanding of how people can lead a successful life with their way of thinking and acting.

Children are encouraged to research definitions of these words for understanding about the significance of their meanings and how they can impact their lives when applied to their mindset.

Mindset Words with…

a

able	achievement
action	accomplish
adapt	adventurous
authentic	activities
awesome	astounding
attitude	altitude

You will be ==able== to ==accomplish== ==amazing== things when you take ==action==. You will have many ==achievements== as you ==adapt== to many ==adventurous activities==. You will learn that it is ==awesome== for you to be your true, ==authentic== self! Your ==altitude== is determined by your ==attitude==.

Mindset Words with…

B

brave	brilliant
balance	better
behavior	boundaries
believable	bright
belong	boost

When you are brave, you don't limit yourself to boundaries that others try to set for you to force you to belong. Your bravery boosts your behavior so that you can become bright and brilliant! You balance yourself for a better life that's believable to you.

Mindset Words with…

c

clever calm
confident connected
conscious creative
clear centered
capable courageous

When you are courageous, it helps you to be confident and capable. When you are conscious of your feelings, your thoughts become clear. You are open to being clever and you use your creativity. Being connected with your thoughts helps you to be centered, balanced, and have a calm demeanor.

Mindset Words with…

D

doer	determination
dedicated	discipline
deliberate	devoted
dynamic	diverse
driven	dependable

When you are a ==doer==, you are ==driven== by ==discipline== to get things done. You are ==dedicated== and ==devoted== toward whatever work you do. You are ==deliberate== in your actions and take on ==diverse== tasks with ==determination==. You become ==dependable==, which allows you to follow through when given responsibilities. All of these help you become a ==dynamic== person.

Mindset Words with…

E

effective eager
excellent engaged
efficient energetic
enthusiastic exceptional
elevated enriching

When you are enthusiastic, you are energetic and eager to do things. You work at an elevated level of being efficient, which causes you to be effective. This leads to your being excellent at what you do. You love to be engaged in enriching activities, and your work is of exceptional quality.

Mindset Words with…

F

fierce	firm
free	fit
flexible	fulfilling
focused	fantastic
favorable	fanatic

When you feel free, it gives you the chance to be flexible and fierce at what you do. You become so focused, you become a fanatic about achieving favorable outcomes. You are firm on doing what you see fit, and you live a fantastic, fulfilling life.

Mindset Words with…

G

greatness	grit
grateful	growth
genuine	gratitude
graceful	generous
gifts	gentle

Greatness comes from striving toward growth. You are a genuine person and generous with your time. You are grateful for your gifts. While you persevere with grit, you are also graceful and gentle with yourself and show gratitude each day for who you are.

Mindset Words with…

H

hard work   honorable
honesty   helpful
heroic   humanity
habits   humor
hopeful   happiness

When you are honorable, you understand your place within humanity comes from being helpful, hopeful, heroic, and honest with yourself and others. You know that happiness comes from being comfortable with who you are, embracing humor to laugh at yourself. You do not walk away from hard work and you live by healthy habits.

Mindset Words with…

I

intelligence   invested
important   integrate
instincts   independent
imagination   integrity
indignant   intuition

In order to be ==independent==, it's ==important== that you are free to ==integrate== your ==intuition== and ==imagination== to build your ==intelligence==. You are ==invested== in trusting your ==instincts== and become ==indignant== when someone challenges your ==integrity==.

Mindset Words with…

J

jovial   judicious
joy   juggle
journey   justify

You find joy when you are able to follow your own journey. You learn to judiciously juggle your actions so that you can continue to strive for jovial outcomes. When you live a life of authenticity, you never need to justify yourself to anyone.

Mindset Words with…

𝒦

keen	knowledge
kindness	acKnowledge
key	asKing
seeK	keep
talKing	knowing

When you seeK knowledge, you become keen at knowing what to do. You acKnowledge that the key to knowing things is to keep asKing questions and talKing about answers. You are strong, and you understand that kindness does not mean you are weak.

Mindset Words with…

L

logical	leader
laugh	learner
like	life
loyal	love
limitless	live

When you are a logical learner, you become a leader. Your opportunities in life are limitless and you love the life you live. You are loyal to your goals and you like to laugh at your mistakes.

Mindset Words with…

M

mindfulness	magnificent
master	manage
mindset	miracle
mystery	mission
magic	mentor

The ==mystery== to having a ==magnificent mindset== is becoming the ==master== of your ==mission==. When you take action, ==miracles== happen, like ==magic==! You become a ==mentor== to others because you know how to ==manage== yourself and your life. You know that your ==mindfulness== leads to success.

Mindset Words with…

𝒩

necessary	notable
natural	never
noble	numerous
navigate	new
noteworthy	nonjudgmental

It is noble to be nonjudgmental. It is necessary to navigate your own natural way to find new opportunities. You will be noteworthy for never giving up, your efforts will be notable, and life will present numerous opportunities for you.

Mindset Words with…

O

opportunities	objective
outstanding	obligated
outgoing	organized
overcome	orderly
outspoken	open-minded

When you are open-minded, you are outgoing about seeking opportunities to grow. You are well organized, orderly, and feel obligated to be outspoken. You are objective about yourself and do outstanding work. You are able to overcome any obstacles that are put in your way.

Mindset Words with…

𝒫

patient persistent
protect perseverance
plans performance
possibilities purpose
pragmatic productive

When you are ==pragmatic==, you look at all ==possibilities== logically and realistically. You are ==patient== with carefully developing your ==plans==, and you act with ==purpose== and ==perseverance==. This allows you to be ==productive== with high ==performance==. You are ==persistent== with your actions and ==protect== yourself from distractions.

Mindset Words with…

Q

question   don't quit
qualify   quality
inQuisitive   acQuire
           quiet

You are a good learner because you are not afraid to question anything to seek or qualify answers. You acQuire knowledge because you are inQuisitive and you refuse to quit. Your work is of the highest quality. You appreciate quiet times knowing that sometimes you need to think before you speak or act.

Mindset Words with…

R

resilient   reliable
rational   reasonable
reflective   respect
receptive   resourceful
responsible   risk

You become successful when you are responsible with everything in your life. You show respect for yourself and you are a reflective thinker. You are reasonable with your thoughts and rational with your actions. You are receptive to other ideas and you are resourceful with your duties. You are not afraid to take risks and you are reliable for others. Most of all, you are resilient because you never give up.

Mindset Words with…

S

skills superior
significant successful
structured strong
stable self-sufficient
strive survive

When you are self-sufficient, you will be successful at things you do. You are not dependent on other people to survive. You are strong and you develop superior skills to complete your work. You put significant effort into everything you do. Your life is structured and stable, and you strive to always do your very best.

Mindset Words with…

T

tenacious   thorough
truthful   thoughtful
timely   thirst
think   try
talk   tell

When you are tenacious, you get things done because you push through to the finish line. You are very thoughtful with your planning. You have a thirst for challenges and your work is very thorough. You think before you act, talk through questions, and are truthful when you tell your answers. You try your best, and you complete tasks in a timely manner.

Mindset Words with...

U

unstoppable
upbeat   unusual
unique   ultimate
uphold   understand

When you are successful, you are ==unstoppable==. You are ==upbeat== and enjoy challenges. You aren't afraid to take on ==unique== and ==unusual== tasks. You ==uphold== the highest standards of work ethics, and ==understand== you must put in the ==ultimate== effort in everything you do.

Mindset Words with…

V

vulnerable   voracious
vigilant   visible
verbalize   various
vary   venture
vested   viable

When you have a vested interest in your various ventures, you are voracious in your efforts to succeed. You are not afraid to be vulnerable and visible in everything you do. You are vigilant at performing your duties and verbalize your needs and concerns for viable solutions. You become laser focused and never vary from your goals.

Mindset Words with…

W

worthy   wonderful
well-cone   winning
welcome   work
wealth   wisdom
worthwhile   willing

When you are willing to welcome wisdom, you will see wonderful outcomes. You focus your hard work on worthwhile actions with a winning attitude. You will be worthy of the wealth that a job well-done will give you.

Mindset Words with…

x

eXcellence   eXample
eXpand   eXciting
eXtreme   eXpectations
eXcuses   eXcel
eXtra   eXtraordinary

You become eXtraordinary when you have high eXpectations and work hard to eXcel at everything you do. You do not make eXcuses and you put in eXtra effort to the eXtreme so that you can eXpand your knowledge and perform with eXcellence. You are eXcited to take on challenges and are an eXample for others to follow.

Mindset Words with…

Y

yield young
yearn yes
yet yourself
yesterday youth

You become successful when you learn from the lessons of your youth. You say "yet" instead of "can't." You use the experiences from yesterday to drive yourself forward for today and tomorrow. You yearn to learn new things, and know that saying "yes to yourself" is what yields new experiences. You know that you are never too young and never too old to learn.

Mindset Words with…

Z

amaZing

When you work hard at everything you do and always put forth your best efforts, you will see amaZing results!

About the Authors

Harry Petsanis is a mindset and accountability coach, philosopher of human nature, consultant, and lifelong fitness and nutrition expert. He is a writer and author, with two published books, "The Truth is A Lie" and "The Logical Path To Life." Harry has a Bachelor's Degree in Journalism, with an intense passion for psychology and the human condition. Harry Petsanis's books are available at Amazon.com.

Donna McCance, M.Ed. is a business administrator, licensed teacher and principal/vice principal with over 20 years experience teaching in elementary education and educational leadership. She has a Masters in Education, Masters in Human Services Management, Bachelors in Business Administration and Associates in Business Administration.

Harry and Donna share a mutual passion for the development of mindset.